MERCUTIO LOVES ROMEO LOVES JULIET LOVES

by Gina Femia

MERCUTIO LOVES ROMEO LOVES JULIET LOVES received its world premiere with Boomerang Theatre Company (Tim Errickson, Artistic Director; Amy Lau Croyle, Associate Producer) at the Jeffrey and Paula Gural Theatre at the A.R.T./New York Theatres. The production ran from November 8th-24th, 2024. It was directed by Scott Ebersold; the set design was by Emmett Grosland; the lighting design was by Derek Van Heel; the costume design was by Brynne Oster-Bainnson; the sound design was by Sam Kaseta; the properties were designed by Kristen VanDerLyn. The production stage manager was Michelle Elizabeth and the assistant stage managers were Rachel McPherson and Rachel Palmer.

The cast was as follows:

ELLIE .... Leah Nicole Raymond

BRITT .... Stacey Raymond

AMBER .... Rocky Vega

ALL RIGHTS RESERVED
Original Works Publishing

CAUTION: Professionals and amateurs are hereby warned that this play is subject to royalty. It is fully protected by Original Works Publishing and the copyright laws of the United States. All rights, including professional, amateur, motion pictures, recitation, lecturing, public reading, radio broadcasting, television, and the rights of translation into foreign languages are strictly reserved.

The performance rights to this play are controlled by Original Works Publishing and royalty arrangements and licenses must be secured well in advance of presentation. No changes of any kind shall be made to the work, including without limitation any changes to characterization, intent, time, place, gender or race of the character. PLEASE NOTE that amateur royalty fees are set upon application in accordance with your producing circumstances. When applying for a royalty quotation and license please give us the number of performances intended, dates of production, your seating capacity and admission fee. Royalty of the required amount must be paid whether the play is presented for charity or gain and whether or not admission is charged. Royalties are payable with negotiation from Original Works Publishing.

Due authorship credit must be given anywhere the title appears, on all programs, printing and advertising for the play. The name of the Playwright must appear on a separate line, in which no other name appears, immediately beneath the title and in size and prominence of type equal to 50% of the largest, most prominent letter used for the title of the Work. No person, firm or entity may receive credit larger or more prominent than that accorded to the Playwright.

Copying from this book in whole or in part is strictly forbidden by law, and the right of performance is not transferable. The purchase of this publication does not constitute a license to perform the work.

Whenever the play is produced, the following notice must appear on all programs, printing, and advertising for the play on separate line:

"**Produced by special arrangement with Original Works Publishing.
www.originalworksonline.com**"

MERCUTIO LOVES ROMEO LOVES JULIET LOVES
© Gina Femia
Trade Edition, 2025
ISBN 978-1-63092-145-3

Also Available From Gina Femia

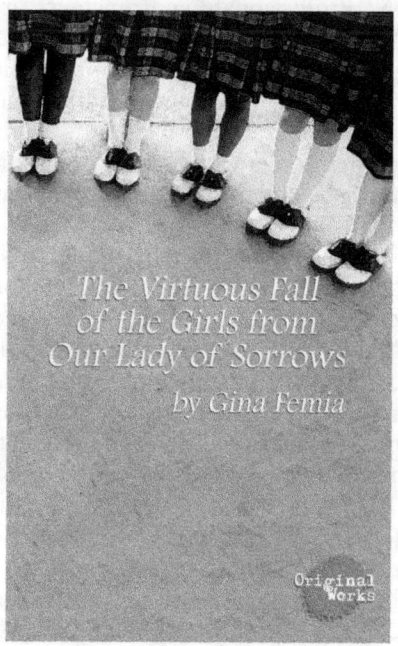

THE VIRTUOUS FALL OF THE GIRLS FROM OUR LADY OF SORROWS
by Gina Femia

Synopsis: At an all-girls Catholic School in East New York, the students of Our Lady of Sorrows are staging an ambitious adaptation of Shakespeare's *Measure for Measure*. As the actors debate the sins of Shakespeare's characters, they question the fundamental tenets of Catholic doctrine, as well as the Church's stance on sexuality, womanhood, and purity. A controversial draft of the play attracts the attention of the nuns and soon the production is in jeopardy. As the girls grapple with faith, love, and adolescence, they find themselves facing off against an oppressive institution.
Cast Size: 7 Females

Folks:

Ellie – serious-minded and doesn't quite know how to fit in, 17
well cast as Mercutio

Britt – all Britt's energy faces forward, falls in love quickly, 17
well cast as Romeo

Amber – a bubbly cheerleader with a huge heart, 17
miscast as Juliet

Setting:

St. William Academy, an All Girls' Catholic School in New Jersey,
mostly in the auditorium that's also a stage that's also a place to dance
and later, Amber's home

And also, it's **2005!**

A note on gender –
These three characters attend an All-Girls' Catholic School in the early 2000s; the world (and more pressingly, their parents) see them as Girls – a label that Ellie and Amber feel comfortable with. Britt is someone who feels less sure about that. Casting should reflect these facts.

A note on age –
Though the characters are seventeen, they can be portrayed by actors of any age. This is a play that plays with the idea of theater – it is a beautiful thing to see older actors inhabit the roles of these younger characters, especially as we watch them grow up in the end. It is also beautiful to see actors closer to the ages of these characters play these roles. Bend age as it suits your production.

Playwrights' Note:
When sentences end without punctuation, there is something unfinished about them. The next sentence does not cut off the first, but comes quickly after.

When (. . . .) appears within a text, a character is searching for language before they speak again.

MERCUTIO LOVES ROMEO LOVES JULIET LOVES

PROLOGUE

(As the lights slowly begin to fade to darkness, we can hear things.
A collage of things,
things that both are real and very much not,
like the sounds of an orchestra starting up,
the sounds of cheerleaders, cheering,
the sounds of someone saying Romeo O Romeo,
the sounds of crickets and birds,
all mixed with the chanting of cheerleading,
the sounds of Shakespeare,
the sounds of 2005
it gets louder and louder,
more and more mashed together until suddenly -)

SCENE I: DRAMA GEEKS V. CHEERLEADERS

(Lights up REAL QUICK and we're in one of those horrible high school bathrooms,
you know the kind, the kind where it's impossible to have a private moment because everything about it's so absolutely public, that kind.
ELLIE and BRITT stand in front of the mirror (which is the audience). They're both wearing School Uniforms (because as if high school's not bad enough, this is an All Girl's Catholic High School), ELLIE is wearing the skirt option, BRITT the slacks. BRITT is holding a piece of scratchy paper towel to her head, ELLIE is trying to help. We're in the middle of it all.)

BRITT: I FUCKING HATE THEM

ELLIE: Calm down!

BRITT: They're such fucking

ELLIE: I know

BRITT: fucking incredibly fucking

ELLIE: Let me see it

BRITT: No but you don't get it

ELLIE: I can't help you if you won't let me SEE

BRITT: I HATE CHEERLEADERS

ELLIE: You've mentioned

BRITT: Fucking walking around like they own the whole school, they don't own shit.

ELLIE: Right

BRITT: Gimme an H! Gimme an A!

ELLIE: I know you're just // spelling Hate,

BRITT: GIMME A T

ELLIE: Stop

BRITT: GIMME AN E

ELLIE: Hate

BRITT: What's that spell?!

ELLIE: You hate cheerleaders!
And guess what, they hate you, too!

BRITT: I didn't even do anything

ELLIE: Sure

BRITT: What, you're on their side?

ELLIE: I'm on your side!
    Yours is the only side I'm on,
    I just also know that I, too, hate cheerleaders,
    But I'm not the one standing here bleeding all over the place

BRITT: It's not
    All over the place

*(ELLIE pats the paper towel on her head.
It's not a huge cut but it's definitely bleeding,
and BRITT accidentally smooshed it so there's blood on her face.)*

ELLIE: Hey.

BRITT: What

ELLIE: Did anybody ever tell you.
    Blood looks good on you

BRITT: Ew, Ellie, shut up

ELLIE: No, what, it does!

BRITT: You're being gross

ELLIE: I'm just saying, you make it work!
    Gonna be the latest fashion trend, in like, Seventeen and YM,
    Blood.
    Everybody's got it

BRITT: Oh please

ELLIE: Not everybody can wear it as good as you, though!

BRITT: God, whatever

(But Britt's laughing. Ellie laughs, too.

*They're quiet as ELLIE runs the water,
starts to wash the blood from her face.
BRITT grabs her wrist awkwardly*

*ELLIE knows it's a hug,
fills her up.*

*They stay like that for a moment.
ELLIE continues to wash BRITT's face.)*

ELLIE: So what happened.

BRITT: Nothing

ELLIE: Uh huh
    but also,
    What really happened?
    Like what actually happened

(Breathing beat.)

BRITT: Katie Gillepski

ELLIE: I knew it

BRITT: Okay so then why'd you make me say it then

ELLIE: 'Cause I want to know what *happened*

BRITT: Fine,
    like, okay.
    I knew the deal.
    Really, I did,
    I knew we were just like…
    hanging out,

that it wasn't like...real.
And it wasn't
but then it was
a little real?
Like, we spent all summer hanging out,
not Being Real together,
like, the whole summer, if I wasn't hanging out with you,
I was hanging out with her
and I thought that maybe it was a little real.
But then school started and she started acting like I was like a
fly,
something she could just swat away.
And I was just walking past her in the hall,
walking past all of them,
they all travel in a pack and said Hi,
I just said hi,
only hi! It just slipped out,
hi,
and she said.
(. . . .)
Like, why say anything to me,
let alone in front of all of - them,
and like.
She was flipping her hair,
she flipped it over her shoulder
and I just
knew that it smelled like butterscotch and firewood
And that pissed me off,
the fact that I know what her hair smells like
because my face was nose deep in her hair while I was
fingering her in the backseat of her mom's Prius,
And she was just
Standing there,
Acting like I was a fly?
Like I was something she could swat?
And I reached over and I
Tugged her hair.

ELLIE: Britt

BRITT: I didn't PULL IT or yank it, I TUGGED IT
   And let go of it and
   Turned around and started walking down the hall
   But fucking Julie S was already chasing after me
   And knocked me down,
   scratched my face
   And called me a.
   Things.

(Another quiet moment between them.)

ELLIE: What things?

BRITT: I don't wanna say them.
   They hurt my brain to think them,
   They'll hurt my tongue to say them.
   And I already hurt so.
   I don't wanna.

(ELLIE puts her arm around BRITT. Pulls BRITT close. BRITT puts her head on ELLIE'S shoulder. It's intimate and sweet.)

ELLIE: This is why you should never trust a cheerleader.

BRITT: Yeah

ELLIE: Always in their dumb packs

BRITT: Like wolves

ELLIE: They are wolves!
   Hey.
   We? Are wolves, too

BRITT: Sure

ELLIE: A pack of wolves

BRITT: Two wolves

ELLIE: Hell yeah

BRITT: Two people can't be a pack, Ellie

ELLIE: We can be!

BRITT: You ever seen anything that's like a pack of something that's only TWO THINGS?

ELLIE: I'm sure there's something

BRITT: Not gum!
Or socks!
Or toilet paper!

ELLIE: No, there's definitely gotta be something

BRITT: Nah, it's more like we're penguins or some shit

ELLIE: A pack of penguins?

BRITT: No, a pair.
Like, the two of us are penguins

ELLIE: No wonder we're fucked against wolves

BRITT: No, but.
We look out for each other.
'Cause we only got each other.

ELLIE: Yeah.
(. . . .)
You know I also heard.
I heard that penguins mate for life.

BRITT: Yeah, everybody knows that

ELLIE: Right

BRITT: That's just like.
  A fact about penguins.
  But it's cool, 'cause. We are.
  Like penguins.

ELLIE: Oh, we.
  We are?

BRITT: Yeah.
  'Cause we're gonna be friends forever, obviously.

ELLIE: Oh, yeah, obviously,
  obviously, yeah.

(BRITT snuggles into Ellie deeper.)

ELLIE: Forever?

BRITT: Yeah, for sure.
  Forever.

(The two do something like a pinkie swear but it's their own swear,
their own finger promise to one another.
BRITT puts her head back on ELLIE's shoulder.
ELLIE smells BRITT's hair.
Closes her eyes.
Holds it inside her.)

BRITT: You're so lucky you're straight

ELLIE : Yeah, for sure.
  I am.
  So lucky.

(They breathe for a moment.)

BRITT: I just hate she did that shit today.
  Gonna be so off my game.

ELLIE: Use it!

BRITT: Yeah, use it

ELLIE: Seriously, though,
   That's like the whole point of acting!
   That you take your bad shit that's happening in your real life and like
   shove it into a fictional person

BRITT: I just hope I get to be Romeo

ELLIE: Oh, you'll be Romeo,
   please, it's like
   no contest!
   You'll be Romeo,
   and I'm gonna be Juliet,
   we're the best actors in the entire school
   AND
   we're seniors,
   literal seniors like,
   what's Sister Magdalene gonna do,
   not cast us?
   Please.
   (. . . .)
   Hey.
   But like.
   Won't it be like.
   Kinda crazy to be like
   Romeo and Juliet?

BRITT: It'll be fun,
   we'd be able to run like
   all our lines together,
   like when I was Peter Pan and you were Wendy -

ELLIE: Totally, totally, yeah, that was great.
   (. . . .)
   But,

it would be like.
Totally weird to like…pretend to be in love, though, right?

BRITT: Oh.
Yeah.
But it would technically be Romeo and Juliet being love, though.

ELLIE: Yeah.
For sure, we'd pretend.

BRITT: Not like we'd have to kiss or anything Sister Magdalene would never let two girls kiss, even if we're just pretending.

ELLIE: Yeah.

(The two of them lapse into silence again.)

ELLIE: You have your monologue ready?

BRITT: Oh, yeah, I'm doing Samwise Gamgee's speech from the Two Towers

ELLIE: What???

BRITT: Yeah

ELLIE: Are you fucking – for real right now??!

BRITT: Yeah, I just got it on DVD

(ELLIE stands abruptly, BRITT kinda falls to the side.)

BRITT: Hey, what the hell!

ELLIE: You're not taking this serious

BRITT: I am so!
   That monologue's so fucking inspirational, are you kidding me?!

ELLIE: Are you kidding me, that's such a bad monologue choice for a classical Shakespeare play!

BRITT: It is not!

ELLIE: It's not even a monologue it's a *speech!*

BRITT: okay, all right, well, what's yours?

ELLIE: The Romeo Romeo monologue

BRITT: That stupid O Romeo monologue?

ELLIE: ...yeah

BRITT: That's going to be *everybody*'s monologue

ELLIE: Yeah but

BRITT: And mine'll be different!
   So see?
   I am taking it serious.

ELLIE: God, whatever.

BRITT: I always take it serious.

(The shrill sound of the late bell breaks through the air. They look at each other.)

ELLIE: All right, well, I guess it's now or never!

BRITT: You nervous?

ELLIE: Nah. You?

BRITT: Never.

ELLIE: Great.

BRITT: Cool.

ELLIE: Let's do this.

*(The two of them do an elaborate handshake.
It starts off pretty chill but keeps building and building, it involves hip bumps and shimmies, and turns into a dance.*

While that's happening, AMBER comes out. She's a cheerleader. She's wearing a cheerleader uniform, the skirt goes to the knees, and also it's not a skirt, it's a skort. She brings the sound of the squad with her, she's surrounded by other cheerleaders, even though we can't see them, we can only see her because she's the only one we need to see.

She's doing a routine. At its height there's some stylized movement where we see her breaking her leg, like, maybe we see AMBER put a boot on herself or something, but what's important is that we just tumble right into the next scene -)

SCENE II: REHEARSAL

(We're in the auditorium, on the multi-function stage and Amber is sitting on a horrible metal folding chair, her broken leg in a brace and up on another awful folding chair. She's still wearing her cheerleading uniform.)

AMBER: oh romeo-romeo
  wait, no.
  okay,
  Oh
  romeo-romeo

(ELLIE enters. Watches AMBER.)

AMBER: no, wait, no okay.
ohromeoromeo

ELLIE: What're you doing?

AMBER: Oh!
Hi!
I didn't realize -
I was just – practicing –
waiting for Britney -

ELLIE: *Britt's* got detention.

AMBER: Oh, yeah, I know!
No, I know,
Sister Magdalene told me and I was like.
Well, may as well practice!
Because like, Berniece has mono and Christina C has mathletes and there's like.
Nobody else who's here that I have scenes with so like.
Here I am!
Practicing!
By myself.

ELLIE: Uh huh

(ELLIE throws her bag down and starts to rummage around in it.)

AMBER: By my…by myself?

ELLIE: Oh yeah, don't mind me.

AMBER: Right but you're. I was just –

ELLIE: I've got Britt's sweater?
And I need to give it back?
So like.
Just ignore me, it's like I'm not even here.

AMBER: But.
    You are here.

ELLIE: Oh my god, so? I'm just one person, what're you gonna do when there's like a million people watching you?

AMBER: Okay.
    Cool, yeah.
    I'll just.
    Don't mind me!

ELLIE: Yeah, I won't.

AMBER: Okay!
    o…kay.
    (beat)
    Oh, Romeo, oh romeo

(ELLIE scoffs.)

AMBER: What?!

ELLIE: Nothing, it's nothing.

AMBER: It's obviously Some-thing

ELLIE: No, no, no,
    it's just.
    Your voice is a little.
    Dead?

AMBER: Is that…a note

ELLIE: No, I mean.
    Maybe…
    Try saying it with.
    Feeling.

AMBER: Okay. OH ROMEO-ROMEO

ELLIE: God, stop you just made your voice Louder

AMBER: So?? That's *feeling*

ELLIE: I can like actually hear the H in your Oh

AMBER: What.

ELLIE: Like, O Romeo Romeo? I can *hear* the H.

AMBER: oh.

ELLIE: O.

AMBER: Oh

ELLIE: O!

AMBER: ...What.

ELLIE: Listen, okay, no offense, like, I think it's great that you're like.
Expanding your horizons,
in this play,
but shouldn't you be.
Rooting for something or something, like you're literally wearing your cheerleading outfit like -

AMBER: Okay, wow, first of all, this? Is a uniform, not an outfit, wow,
and Yeah, I should be but I can't and I need an after school activity to keep my fucking scholarship and this is the only -
It's not my fault I broke my leg!

ELLIE: Isn't it, though?
A little?
Like, if you're a cheerleader, shouldn't you like.
Not fall?

AMBER: No.
 That's stupid.
 That's like saying You're an actor so you shouldn't forget your lines

ELLIE: Oh my god, you SHOULDN'T FORGET YOUR LINES

AMBER: God, whatever,
 Katie Gillepski fucked a pass and -
 Not that it's literally any of your business.
 I'm not supposed to like blame anyone but she did and it sucks and now I'm out of the whole season my senior year
 MY SENIOR YEAR, god! It sucks.
 Because I'd definitely rather be cheering more than anything else in the entire fucking world.

(ELLIE rolls her eyes, busies herself.)

AMBER: Also sometimes actors? Do forget their lines.

(ELLIE ignores her.)

AMBER: Besides cheerleading is like.
 All falling.
 So you're wrong about that, too.

ELLIE: Yeah, well I wouldn't know.
 I could never really get into cheerleading.
 Power tripping's not really my thing.

AMBER: I don't power trip! Jesus. That's gross, shit.

ELLIE: Sure.

AMBER: No, I mean, yeah, I feel powerful.
 But not like, over people.
 I just Feel Powerful.

Using my whole voice?
There's not a lot of places you could use your voice,
your whole voice,
have it fill an entire space.
Like, we're supposed to walk around all quiet and shit,
like, if we shout in the halls we get detention
'cause it's not ladylike to shout,
but it's impossible to be quiet when you're cheering.
You need to be loud and like
as a big as possible,
Like my face?
Has to take up my entire face, like
(She smiles huge,
makes big motions with her mouth,
her face takes up her entire face.)
And when I'm in the air,
My body has to take up all the space in the air,
and it's not like flying
because if I was flying, I'd be able to stay up there forever,
it's falling.
All Falling.

(There's an awkward silence. ELLIE looks at her script.
Can't read any of the words.
Looks at the sky, back at the script.)

ELLIE: That's…kinda like acting.
    The being loud?
    And big?
    Except you have to take the quiet emotions
    and make them loud and big.

AMBER: Sounds (. . . .) impossible.

ELLIE: Well, it's not, it's literally what acting is so it's like.
    Literally possible so. *(beat)* You know, I wanted to be Juliet.

AMBER: Oh. That's why you're so much – this

ELLIE: I'm not anything!

AMBER: Sure

ELLIE: Just weird that you're like.
Not very good at this and that somehow you got the best part in the play,
that's all.
Almost like cheerleaders always get special treatment or something, I dunno.

(They fall into silence again.)

AMBER: Sister Magdalene probably cast you as Mercutio because your audition was the only funny one.

ELLIE: No it wasn't

AMBER: Yeah, I didn't even know what you were saying but it was like. Funny.

ELLIE: She made me read the Mercutio sides. I didn't wanna

AMBER: Because you knew she'd cast you

ELLIE: I just (. . . .) really wanted to be Juliet.

(Another awkward moment.)

AMBER: You are really good, you know.

ELLIE: Oh, nah

AMBER: Yeah, I've. I've actually seen like all the plays

ELLIE: Oh, well. I have been in them all.

AMBER: You were a really good Antigone

ELLIE: Yeah, well. That was a great role.

AMBER: Yeah but you were. Really good. (. . . .)
　　Mercutio's the harder part, I think.
　　'Cause like.
　　Anyone can be Juliet.
　　But not anyone could be Mercutio.

(ELLIE pretends to not hear that.
But she hears it and might remember it for the rest of her life.
She smiles.
AMBER holds ELLIE's smile in her face.
She has a nice smile.
BRITT interrupts, entering with all the energy in the world.)

BRITT: Seriously FUCK detention

ELLIE: Detention ended a million years ago, where the fuck've you been

BRITT: Uh, I had to get chips??, here *(Throws a small bag at Ellie.)*
　　I was fucking starving,
　　the whole time I was there I was just thinking about chips,
　　Actually, no, I was thinking about Doritos, the Cool Ranch ones?
　　I just couldn't stop thinking about Doritos,
　　Doritos, just racing through my mind,
　　so then Father Chris was like Okay, you can go
　　and I ran to the vending machine,
　　but it wasn't taking dollars! Only change!
　　Like, what! The fuck,
　　so I had to go to Donnie's Deli and they were outta

    Doritos so I just got chips
(Obnoxiously chews the chips.)

AMBER: Doritos are a type of chip

BRITT: Yeah but they *aren't chips*, you know?

ELLIE: Yeah, seriously, they're Doritos??

AMBER: Okay.

BRITT: Yo, yo, who am I

(Britt does something gross, like shows the gross chewed up chips in her mouth and does something like inside-jokey, like makes a face or a sound or something that cracks ELLIE up, the two of them having a whole conversation without words, having a moment that's so insular it almost physically hurts to watch.)

AMBER: I'm Amber by the way.

BRITT: Yeah, I know who you are.
    We've had French together for like.
    Every year.

AMBER: Yeah, but I never like.
    Introduced myself
    so. Hi.

BRITT: Hello.

(beat)

ELLIE: Hey, let's get pizza

BRITT: K.

AMBER: But. Rehearsal's still. Happening?

BRITT: Yeah but I missed most of it.

ELLIE: Yeah

BRITT: So like. See you tomorrow.

AMBER: All right well -

(The two leave.)

AMBER: Oh-kay.

(Amber starts to pack up and leave, too but stops. Picks up her script. Opens her mouth to read from it again instead and the scene shifts into -)

SCENE III: MIRROR MIRROR

(The next day. BRITT and AMBER are standing in the middle of the space, playing the mirror game with each other. AMBER is wearing her cheerleading uniform. BRITT is committed to be a professional in this moment even though she'd rather be playing the mirror game with anybody else. BRITT is obviously leading and AMBER hesitantly follows. Britt makes a big, weird funny face but Amber does a half-assed cringe version of that face. Britt drops the game, annoyed.)

BRITT: Oh, come on

AMBER: What, I did it!

BRITT: You did not, I did this *(Makes the face)* and you did *(Amber's version.)*

AMBER: I just, this is really (. . . .) I hate this!

BRITT: It's just a game

AMBER: Yeah, ok, if it's just a game, then why isn't it fun?

BRITT: It's fun! You're thinking too hard

AMBER: You can't think *too hard*, that isn't a thing

BRITT: It 100 percent is a thing

AMBER: What's the point of this stupid game, anyway?

BRITT: It's so we can be in sync and like read each other's minds or something. Like, we're Romeo and Juliet and need to like. Be in sync.

AMBER: Why, we're barely even in any scenes together

BRITT: Yeah but.
    The play's called Romeo & Juliet?
    So like…
    I dunno, Ellie explains it better than me.
    Come on.

(Britt starts again. Amber half-heartedly follows again.
The two are pretty in sync for a moment.
While they're still doing their movements.)

AMBER: Ellie's like. Really good at all this

BRITT: Yeah, she is.
    I mean, so am I, obviously but like.
    Ellie wants to be an actor for real so she knows more stuff.

(They're in sync for a moment.)

AMBER: You're cast as a guy a lot

(BRITT drops the game, defensive.)

BRITT: Yeah, so what?

AMBER: Nothing, I was just saying -

BRITT: I like it. Like, if I had to be Juliet and wear a dress?
Gross.
But being a guy, it's, I dunno.
It's fun.
And I'm good at it. So?

(Starts leading the game again, a little more aggressive than before.)

AMBER: Ellie didn't wanna be cast as a guy

BRITT: She's just bummed she's not the lead. But you know what they say. There are some small parts and there are some big parts, but actors have to act them!

(AMBER gives BRITT a look like does anybody say that? BRITT's like, people say that all the time. They go back to the game. AMBER messes up again, BRITT breaks the game, annoyed.)

BRITT: Okay, I know what this is.

(BRITT walks away from AMBER.)

AMBER: What?

BRITT: You don't wanna do this with me because I'm gay

AMBER: What? No, I just suck at this!

BRITT: Sure, it's just that nobody's ever been this bad at this game in the history of this game existing, you just don't wanna look me in the eye and shit

AMBER: I literally don't care that you're gay

BRITT: And the play's gonna suffer because you can't even look at me // you can't even look -

AMBER: No, for real,
I don't care, Britt,
I'm actually,
I'm, I'm bi.

(BRITT's worldview is kinda shattered.)

BRITT: You……are?

AMBER: Yeah.

BRITT: Seriously? I mean…the cheerleaders? they know?

AMBER: Oh, uh yeah –

BRITT: Because they're a little.
A lot with the.
They kinda hate…

AMBER: Yeah, but it's just like…
They don't really…
Like, I told them I was bi last year and they were kinda like 'Oh yeah, sure you are, Amber,' and they kinda just…ignored it?
But then this summer, I was hanging out with this guy, he goes to St. Tim's?
Like, we spent almost everyday together, just chillin' and sometimes we'd make out and like
a couple of times we kinda, you know, we fucked
I mean, it was like, there was nothing better to do, you know?
Like, TV's all reruns in the summer.

BRITT: Yeah, no, right

AMBER: And I mean, I liked it, it was fun,
But he started calling me his girlfriend?
And I thought that was weird because I didn't even like him like that,
but he was calling me his girlfriend,
and I realized that I didn't really wanna do things together, like go on dates or hold hands or talk about life, I'd rather just fuck once in a while.
But the cheerleaders, they found out about it and they were like
so excited I had a boyfriend?
They were all,
'See, Amber, we knew you were just confused!'
So it's like.
Because I've only ever had a…been with him, they don't think I'm really -
they don't think it counts and they don't believe? me?
That I am.
I mean, who does, everything's like.
Being bi doesn't exist or count or is real
even though I'm Real and…
It's fine it just also sucks?
It sucks, it
whatever, it's (. . . .) So yeah, I literally don't care you're gay.
Let's just.

(AMBER holds up her hands with new determination.)

BRITT: Why do you put up with the cheerleaders if they're like that?

AMBER: Because. Like, what choice do I have?
I love cheer.
And when we're out there, practicing, performing, it almost feels like.
Maybe it could be different.

(AMBER puts her hands up again. BRITT thinks about saying something else, but doesn't.
Puts down the backpack. Crosses back to AMBER. They start playing the game again, leading as AMBER follows.)

SCENE IV: LET'S TALK ABOUT

(Rehearsal, after school. ELLIE and BRITT sit together, making headstones out of cardboard boxes. They're in the middle of an important conversation.)

ELLIE: Come on, it's a great idea

BRITT: It's okay

ELLIE: It's genius, pure genius!

BRITT: I mean – I guess

ELLIE: Imagine, just picture it,
October 28th
seven o'clock pm.
The Halloween Dance is in full swing,
all the cheerleaders already at their stupid dance stations, dishing out the fruit punch and making sure people don't eat all their stupid cookies
when all of a sudden there's a fog

BRITT: where the hell're we getting *fog*

ELLIE: and outta that fog, what appears but Two
ZOMBIE CHEERLEADERS

(ELLIE does some zombie moves, complete with zombie sounds, the type a zombie cheerleader may make specifically. BRITT's like I mean, this is amusing but I really don't wanna do it.)

ELLIE: Katie Gillepski will shit herself, she'll be so pissed but she won't be able to do anything because we'll be at the dance.

BRITT: How're we even gonna get the uniforms

ELLIE: I already got them! They keep extras in the same closet they keep the Jesus wine, come on, Britt, why're you being so weird about this??

BRITT: I'm not being weird

ELLIE: You so are, don't you wanna like stick it to the cheerleaders?

BRITT: Obviously! I just (....) don't wanna wear a skirt.

ELLIE: It's not a skirt, it's a skort

BRITT: Same shit!

ELLIE: Well we've gotta figure it out, the dance is in three weeks!

(She goes back to making her grave, a little aggressively.)

ELLIE: I bet Katie goes as something stupid like
a sexy cat
which is so unfair to cats everywhere

(AMBER enters. She's wearing headphones and pretending to listen to a discman, holding a bunch of stuff to make graves in her arms. She's wearing her cheer uniform and the boot.)

ELLIE: Speaking of zombie cheerleaders.

(BRITT laughs along but also gives AMBER a kinda half-nod thing that ELLIE doesn't see.

AMBER pretends to ignore them both, begins making her own graves.)

BRITT: You think they'll use some of our graves to decorate for the dance?

ELLIE: They better not

BRITT: Why, they're really good!

ELLIE: Because these are for the play, not the dance.

BRITT: Yeah, but look, check this out *(holds up a grave)* R.I.P. Rock Hard. You get it?

ELLIE: Yeah, I mean, there's like. Not much to Get

BRITT: It's a good one

ELLIE: It's obvious

BRITT: Yeah but that's what makes it hilarious!

ELLIE: Also, I don't know anyone whose name is Rock. So it doesn't work.

BRITT: Whatever, it's funny, I think it's funny

ELLIE: Sister Magdalene's never gonna let you put it out there

BRITT: She's not gonna get it, she's a nun

ELLIE: Nuns know about rock hard, Britt, please

BRITT: How

ELLIE: Are you serious – they're not like in a sexless void, like, she lives out in the world, you know?

BRITT: God, whatever.

(They go back to making the graves.)

AMBER: What if you did a name like. Richard Head.

BRITT: What?

AMBER: Because that's one that you've gotta.
    You gotta think about it,
    you know?

(BRITT and ELLIE don't really get it.)

AMBER: You know.
    Richard?
    And then Head?

(They get it.)

BRITT: Oh shit, that is a good one

AMBER: Yeah, it's deep, right?

BRITT: It's got layers

ELLIE: God, whatever.

(They continue making graves.)

BRITT: Hey. It's crazy that Romeo and Juliet only got married so they could fuck, right?

ELLIE: That's not the only reason

AMBER: It's the Mostly reason

ELLIE: People back then didn't like go on dates and stuff,
    they got married

and half the time it wasn't even because they loved each other
or liked each other,
it was all like politics and shit

AMBER: well they liked and loved each other and definitely wanted to fuck so

BRITT: bet they didn't even do anything fancy,
just like
missionary

ELLIE: yeah okay

BRITT: What

ELLIE: what do you know about fancy sex

AMBER: missionary's not that boring

ELLIE: what

AMBER: like, missionary's actually,
it's fun
I mean, all it means is that like.
One person's on top and you can make eye contact during it if you wanna, you know?

(They consider this. Continue making headstones.)

BRITT: Hey. Do you think their sex was like. Good?

(ELLIE starts to answer but is cut off by AMBER.)

AMBER: Probably not if it was like
the one time,
you need to do it at least like five times for it to get good –

BRITT: like three times

AMBER: right, it depends

ELLIE: It doesn't matter!
　　Like it's not real sex, it's a play,
　　it's metaphor sex!
　　Imagination sex,
　　it's not even actually in the play

BRITT: So?

ELLIE: I dunno, I just think it's whatever!

(Another making graves beat. BRITT gets an idea.)

BRITT: Hey.
　　How many fingers have you ever.
　　You know.
　　Gotten up there.

ELLIE: We shouldn't be – Sister Magdalene can walk in here, any minute -

AMBER: Which hole

BRITT: Either

AMBER: Three. You?

BRITT: Like.
　　I dunno.
　　Like.
　　On me?
　　I dunno, like *(Britt switches between 3 and 4 fingers, 3 and 4, 3? No, definitely, 4 definitely...mmm, no, maybe 3...)*

ELLIE: Oh my god, how don't you know?!

BRITT: I'm not exactly documenting shit when I do it! God!

AMBER: You know Julie S? Cheerleader?

BRITT: Yeah, unfortunately

AMBER: She uses a cucumber.

(Beat. What?!)

ELLIE: No she doesn't

AMBER: I've seen it

ELLIE & BRITT: WHAT?!

AMBER: When we went over her house for a sleepover, she showed us

BRITT: Like a fresh cucumber?!

AMBER: Sometimes

ELLIE: SOMETIMES

AMBER: I mean, she has to replace it!
It's produce, you know?
She calls it Mr. Cucumber

BRITT: You're lying

AMBER: I'm not

BRITT: So if I went up to Julie S and asked her –

AMBER: I mean, I wasn't supposed to.
Don't do that though?
Like, she wouldn't…
Uh.

(Beat. It sinks in. She turned on the cheerleaders. Respect.)

BRITT: A cucumber.

AMBER: Yeah.

BRITT: Huh. I've never thought to use food

AMBER: She says it's like. Really good

(They all think about that.)

BRITT: What'd it. Did you smell it

ELLIE: Okay, stop,
   Stop!
   I'm done with –
   We're making graves,
   so like, let's just.
   Let's do that.
   Okay?

(Beat.)

AMBER: It smelled like Cheetos and maple syrup

BRITT: Oh my god, I know exactly how that smells like

ELLIE: I'm going to VOM EVERYWHERE

BRITT: You're such a prude Ellie

ELLIE: I am not! You know I'm not

BRITT: What, because of the tampon –

ELLIE: No, not –
   I'm not talking about –
   But also, I did!

When I took it out, I had .... an orgasm —
But no, I didn't mean, I meant -
the shower noz —
My mom has this shower nozzle?
So like.
You know.
That's what I use.
When I need to. You know.
Do that.
And it works, too.
So yeah, I'm not a prude.
I just.
A cucumber is.
A waste of food.

BRITT: Uh huh

ELLIE: Well you can't put it in a salad afterward, Britt!

BRITT: Doesn't mean it's not serving a purpose!

AMBER: I mean, but.
You technically could.
Put it in a salad?
it's all natural, you know?

ELLIE: Stop, stop, I don't wanna talk about -
Like, let's talk about death!
Everybody in this play dies!
If we're gonna talk about anything, let's just talk about death,
okay?

AMBER: It's weird though that like.
We can talk about death and like
you know, you get stabbed and like Tybalt gets
stabbed and we've already had all those meetings
about what to make the blood outta to make it the like
right kinda looking blood and stuff but we can't talk
about sex and that's like a worse sin than murder.
You know?

(Beat. Yeah, that is weird. AMBER shrugs, goes to put her headphones back on.)

BRITT: Hey. What're you listening to?

AMBER: Oh, just a mix CD? I burned it myself. It's all random songs, like it's got "Crazy in Love" and like "Since You've Been Gone" and then like, I dunno, "Defying Gravity"

ELLIE: From *Wicked*?!

AMBER: Yeah

ELLIE: I LOVE that song

AMBER: I know, it's so good, right?!

BRITT: What, what song

AMBER: Oh my god, you don't know it?!

ELLIE: I've been telling you to listen to it –

AMBER: Oh my god, I can't believe you don't know it!

BRITT: I don't really Do Showtunes!

AMBER: Yeah but it like, it's not like a regular showtune, it, it like –

ELLIE: transcends the genre!

AMBER: Yes! Yes, exactly, it transcends the -

ELLIE: Here, play it, play it, get it –

AMBER: No, I know, I'm looking –

BRITT: Oh my god there's no way this song is that good

ELLIE & AMBER: Yes it is, are you kidding me?!

AMBER: Here, HERE!

(AMBER shoves the headphones onto BRITT's head. BRITT can smell her body wash.
Like vanilla and the ocean.
BRITT listens to the song. ELLIE and AMBER watch BRITT listen. They're really excited.)

ELLIE: Oh my god, I wish we could hear it, too

AMBER: I know, right? It's so good

ELLIE: It really is

(Small watching beat.)

AMBER: You know, I heard that Britney Spears watched Wicked and it changed her life

ELLIE: No way

AMBER: Her *whole life*

ELLIE: No

AMBER: Yeah, she saw it last year and then she was like 'I'm changing my whole life, I'm leaving singing behind to become a scientist'

ELLIE: She did not

AMBER: No, for real, she did!

ELLIE: So she's a scientist now?!

AMBER: I mean, I dunno, but like she wrote she wanted to be

(BRITT makes a sudden movement. The two stop, bated breath – is the song over?! No, not yet.)

AMBER: Like, imagine,
 being one of the biggest singers in the world and then like,
 seeing a play,
 seeing Wicked,
 and realizing that like wow.
 I don't wanna do this anymore,
 That's like.
 Big.
 Like, it's just a play.
 How could a play change your whole life, you know?

(But AMBER notices that ELLIE isn't listening. Because ELLIE is watching BRITT. AMBER watches ELLIE watch BRITT. Nudges her.)

AMBER: Hey, do you like Britt…tney Spears?

ELLIE: Not really. Her songs are mostly too happy

AMBER: What's wrong with being happy?

ELLIE: Nothing's wrong with it.
 But it's like.
 Hard to hear. Sometimes.

(BRITT takes the headphones off.)

ELLIE: Well?

AMBER: What'd you think?!

(BRITT doesn't say anything. Maybe just clears her throat a few dozen times, trying not to cry.)

BRITT: I'm just. That was (. . . .) I wanna listen again.

ELLIE: Wait, I wanna hear it, too!

AMBER: Me, TOO! Here, come on –

(The three crowd around the discman. BRITT holds up the headphones in the center.
AMBER turns the volume up as high as it'll go. The tinny sound of the song comes through the headphones. The three listen together as we move into -)

SCENE V: CRAMPS

(The rehearsal space, the next day. The headstones are stacked in a corner. There are some more props around, too. ELLIE enters the rehearsal room. She's all hunched over in pain.
Maybe moans a bit in that helpless way, in that Ouch, I have cramps and this sucks so much but there's nothing I can really do to make them cease but moan! – way.
Pushes together a few chairs, making a bit of a chair bench. Drapes herself over them. Closes her eyes and moans some more. AMBER enters. She's wearing her cheer uniform, boot's still on her leg. Sees ELLIE. Approaches cautiously.)

AMBER: Hey.
    Are you.
    Alive?

ELLIE: No

AMBER: Oh no

ELLIE: I have cramps and I wanna die

AMBER: Oh yeah, that sucks.
    Moving around's supposed to help,
    like walking?
    I read about it in Seventeen -

ELLIE: I don't wanna move, I wanna become fused to the chair

AMBER: That sounds uncomfortable. To be a chair forever?

ELLIE: I guess.

AMBER: Butts all over you,

ELLIE: That's not so bad

AMBER: Farting on you

ELLIE: ew

AMBER: I'm sorry you hurt

ELLIE: Thanks.

AMBER: Do you know where Britt is?

ELLIE: Detention.

AMBER: Again?

ELLIE: Yeah.
Britt gets detention a lot.
You should just like.
Use the time to memorize your lines or something.

AMBER: Yeah. *(She picks up her script. Looks at it.)*
There's just like. So many lines.

ELLIE: I already memorized all mine

AMBER: How

ELLIE: I only have 62, so. It was easy

AMBER: Sure. *(She looks at the script. Back at ELLIE.)* Hey. Did you really have an orgasm when you took out your tampon

ELLIE: Yes! I did! I really did! I dunno why that's so unbelievable a thing!

AMBER: I dunno. Maybe because. Of all the blood?

ELLIE: It was only the one time but it happened and it was awkward because I was at my cousin's confirmation and I was in the bathroom where all the priests go and I had an orgasm in a place of God and it happened and that's why I switched to pads.

AMBER: Okay. *(Looks at the script. Back to ELLIE.)* Hey, do you like. Have any advice? On how to memorize all this? You just. Seem to really know what you're doing and I...I dunno...

ELLIE: Oh. Uh, yeah, sure.
Try saying your lines out loud
Like, talk them out loud,
It helps.
Makes them more real 'cause it's in your mouth, and your mouth is real, you know?

AMBER: Oh. Didn't think of that. (. . . .) Thanks. Thanks for. (. . . .) You sure I'm not gonna like, disturb you?

ELLIE: Not unless you're my uterus

AMBER: Okay, okay, cool. Cool. *(Clears her throat. Regards her script.)*
Oh, Romeo. Romeo, Where............the fuck,
I hate this,
I dunno what I'm saying,
what the hell am I saying?! And who am I talking to, why am I talking, like, nobody does that in real life, I

mean, yeah, okay I'll say things like out loud to myself sometimes but not like a whole entire block of text, who am I talking to?? Why am I talking?!

ELLIE: Okay, wow, breathe first of all.

AMBER: I dunno why she made me Juliet, I shouldn't be Juliet, she has too many lines, look at all these lines, what do they mean, what do they mean?!

ELLIE: All right, well,
you are Juliet?
So like, you don't have a choice

AMBER: I can quit

ELLIE: And secondly, yeah, I know this is all written like, weird it's poetry, like nobody actually talked like this ever in the history of the world for real, that's why it's harder to understand, but it's like. Because. You love Romeo

AMBER: Yeah, I got that

ELLIE: And like love?
Is so big!
And weird!
And makes no sense.
So it's like the only way to talk about it is to make it larger than life.
And in this moment,
right here, in this very moment,
Juliet, she's like
Never been in love before.
And she's In Love.
So she's talking because it's just too big to keep it inside,
Too large for her thoughts,
She has to say it out loud,
To the sun, to the sky to the world.

(AMBER is looking at ELLIE. She has fallen in love.)

AMBER: O.

ELLIE: That help?

AMBER: Yeah. Kinda, it does.

ELLIE: Cool.

AMBER: You…really are good at all this

ELLIE: Yeah, well. I love it.

AMBER: Like. Shakespeare?

ELLIE: I dunno, just like Drama in general?
It's like.
All fake but also not really.
It's just.
Always been a place where I felt like I could breathe?
Sorry, that probably sounds – stupid

AMBER: No, I get it.

ELLIE: Really?

AMBER: Yeah. There's not a lotta places where it feels like. Good to breathe.

ELLIE: Yeah.

(The two share a moment.)

ELLIE: You know I actually – I made a discovery.
About the play.

AMBER: Oooh what?

ELLIE: I dunno, it might – it might sound stupid

AMBER: It won't

ELLIE: It might

AMBER: Nothing you say ever sounds stupid

(A moment. Ellie takes a deep breath.)

ELLIE: Okay, well, I think -

(But whatever she's going to say is cut off. BRITT enters with energy like a thunderstorm, throws her backpack across the stage.)

ELLIE: Yo, what's wrong

BRITT: Fucking nothing

ELLIE: Yeah okay

BRITT: Just. Had detention

ELLIE: And? What's wrong?

AMBER: Yeah, what'd you do?

BRITT: Nothing.
    I didn't do anything.
    I just.
    Told Sister Rose that she sucks.

AMBER: Seriously?

BRITT: Yeah well I only said it because she sucks

ELLIE: She does suck

BRITT: Right!
    And she was talking about that new rule, thing.
    About how – the dance that.
    The no dancing thing.

ELLIE: Ooooh.

BRITT: Yeah and I was like
in Lit and everyone was talking about it and I was like
It's stupid,
Because it is stupid,
girls should be able to dance with each other,
like, as friends, even,
friendship dancing is a thing!
But then it was like no,
it's so atrocious a thought,
so unbearably gay a thought,
and Sister Rose gave me that look that she always gives me,
concern and like
pity,
and so I told her she sucks,
even though I didn't even mean her,
not just her,
I meant.
It all.
And a little bit her specifically.

ELLIE: She does suck

AMBER: Uber sucks

BRITT: Whatever.

*(ELLIE holds BRITT's hand.
Squeezes it. It's so intimate and deep, AMBER doesn't know what to do.)*

AMBER: Hey.
I was just like,
running lines,
practicing the Balcony Scene?

BRITT: Oh, I'm in that one

ELLIE: Yup, obviously. It's only. Iconic

AMBER: Let's run it

BRITT: I dunno

AMBER: Come on, I'll even like. Stand on the balcony.

ELLIE: There's no balcony –

AMBER: Sure there is! You already made the balcony, look!

(AMBER points to the chair bench. They all stare at it for a few seconds.)

AMBER: Here, help me up

BRITT: Aren't you like…maimed?

AMBER: I'll do it myself if you don't help –

(She starts to try to get ontop of the chair.)

BRITT: Yo, I really think you should probably remain seated?

AMBER: How're we supposed to do the balcony scene without a balcony?!

ELLIE: God, with imagination?!

AMBER: This is imagination! It's not a real balcony, it's chairs! You gonna help me or what?

(ELLIE starts to move towards her, but BRITT pushes her out of the way.)

BRITT: Okay –

(BRITT takes AMBER's hand. It's deep and intimate. Britt has fallen in love.)

AMBER: Everything okay?

BRITT: Yeah, for sure.
　I've just.
　I never noticed, your eyes,
　They're like
　so……wet?

AMBER & ELLIE: What?

BRITT: I mean, damp,
　moist?
　I've just.
　Never seen eyes like yours. Before.

(Another weird tense moment.)

ELLIE: Okay, then…you both should do the balcony scene and.

(ELLIE starts to leave.)

AMBER: Wait –
　Can you like.
　Stay?

ELLIE: Really?

AMBER: Yeah it'd be like. Good to have your eyes on this scene.

*(ELLIE hesitates. Puts her bag back down. She watches as they do the balcony scene.
It's silent. It transports us into –)*

SCENE VI: ARE YOU GOING TO THE DANCE?

(Play rehearsal, Friday afternoon. ELLIE and BRITT are in the middle of an important conversation.)

BRITT: You need to practice it, too

ELLIE: Yeah, but I don't wanna

BRITT: Come on, just run it with me!

ELLIE: You're not Tybalt -

BRITT: It's literally the same choreo for your fight! All the fights are the same! Sister Magdalene made all the fights the same, come on, just do it with me

ELLIE: God, fine.

(ELLIE and BRITT practice a sword fight. The one where Romeo fights Tybalt and then Tybalt dies, They're practicing that fight. BRITT's kinda all over the place.)

ELLIE: Wait, stop, stop, Wow, you really are bad at this

BRITT: I know, I dunno where to put my arm and my hand and my foot and my sword -

ELLIE: All right, come on, here, Let's do it without the swords, just focus on the footwork.

(ELLIE throws her prop sword down. BRITT does, too. And it is like a dance, a sweet little dance, how much of it is the fight and how much of it is a dance that they start to do? It's a mix,

                    playing,
                    dancing,
                    fighting.

AMBER enters, sees it. Her heart feels something. She interrupts their dance.)

AMBER: Ellie? Sister's ready for you

ELLIE: Yeah, cool, gotta go get killed

BRITT: Say hi to the Devil for me

(Does a weird Devil thing and ELLIE does one back before she leaves.)

BRITT: All right, so hey, do you wanna do the holy Palmers stuff? I think we should practice the Holy Palmers – *(Rifles through the script.)*

AMBER: Yeah, yeah sure - hey, can I ask you a question?

BRITT: Yeah, of course, anything

AMBER: What's Ellie's like…deal?

BRITT: Deal?

AMBER: Yeah, like what's she into?

BRITT: Oh, I dunno, regular stuff, I guess? Like, manga, musicals, *America's Next Top Model*

AMBER: No, I mean like – you know, what kinda people does she like?

BRITT: Oh, I dunno. She talks about Leonardo DiCaprio a lot

AMBER: What about. Is she into…girls?

BRITT: Ellie? Oh, no, she's straight, she's so straight, like if straight people had a mascot, they'd be Ellie

AMBER: Oh. Are you sure?

BRITT: Yeah, of course, I'm her best friend, I would know.

AMBER: Right

BRITT: Me, though, I'm gay

AMBER: No, right, right I know! I know.

(AMBER looks at her script. BRITT pretends to look at the script but really looks at AMBER.)

BRITT: Hey, are you. You going to the dance tomorrow? Or are you gonna have to sit it out because of – *(Gestures to the boot.)*

AMBER: Oh, no, this actually comes off tomorrow

BRITT: That's cool! You'll be able to really like (. . . .) cut a rug *(Does a cringe dance move. BRITT tries to recover.* Or are you, probably gonna be helping out the cheerleaders -

AMBER: Oh, no.
    I was supposed to but.
    I just.
    I'm not gonna.

BRITT: Cool. That's cool.

AMBER: You got your costume ready and everything?

BRITT: Yeah, kinda.
    I don't really wanna wear it though.
    It's – there's a skirt involved,
    or well, I guess it's technically a skort
    but yeah I don't wanna wear it.

AMBER: So wear something else

BRITT: I dunno if I should even go, the whole no
dancing thing

AMBER: It's so shitty

BRITT: Yeah

AMBER: That's actually....It was the cheerleaders, their
idea?

BRITT: Are you fuckin' for real?

AMBER: Yeah. That's why I'm not helping them.
They told some of the Sisters that some girls were
planning on going together, like as couples
and I told them it was dumb and they were like
whatever, Amber, you're just confused
and it just sucks because I love cheer
but I hate them
and I guess they hate me, too.
I guess they always have.

BRITT: That really – it sucks

AMBER: So yeah, I'm not gonna help them.

BRITT: It's so stupid, they act like it's just a phase, like
it's something that'll just float right outta us if only we
pray hard enough and it's not true, it's just not true.

AMBER: Yeah, like, I go to church all the time so like if
Jesus wanted me to be straight, wouldn't he have, I
dunno, zapped me with some Jesus-Superpower by
now or something?

(BRITT laughs.)

BRITT: Jesus-Superpower?

AMBER: Well, I dunno! He made water turn into wine, and like rose from the literal dead so.
Seem like superpower shit to me!

BRITT: Yeah, I guess you're right.

AMBER: Church sucks.

BRITT: I stopped going

AMBER: Lucky. My parents won't let me, they like. Force me to go. Even though I don't wanna.

BRITT: Oh, yeah.
Yeah.
I mean – it's not.
I kinda, I miss going.
To church.

AMBER: Really?!

BRITT: Yeah, no, I don't mean –
I don't miss, like
going-going, I miss.
Going.
Like, being inside a church.
The quiet smell of incense and the smooth wooden pews,
it's like being inside a castle,
and sometimes,
I used to go inside and just sit,
when it wasn't Sunday,
I'd go inside and sit so still,
I could feel my heart   beat inside my body,
but when they talk about,
what they think about.
Me.
It kinda. It sucks.
Because

They hate (. . . .) me, even with all the words they use to
doll it up, doesn't change the fact that they hate (. . . .)
Me. And that.
Sucks.
They took my castle away.
I'm tired of them taking things away from me.
From us.

(BRITT's in the feels. AMBER's getting pissed.)

AMBER: Hey.
    We should like.
    Do something at the dance.
    I've kinda got an idea.

BRITT: What kinda idea?

AMBER: A good one. You trust me?

(Amber holds out a pinky. BRITT hesitates, returns the swear. As they do, the pulsing beat of some dance music starts to play as we move into -)

SCENE VII: AT THE HALLOWEEN DANCE

(Saturday night at the dance! It's in that same auditorium, but there are orange and black streamers, maybe a skull or two. ELLIE is dressed like a Zombie Cheerleader. She's wearing the same kinda uniform that the school uses and has done her make up to look Zombie-like. She's looking at her gigantic cellphone, looking up, she's waiting for somebody. BRITT enters. She's dressed like Romeo. Goes up to ELLIE.)

BRITT: Yo!

ELLIE: Oh! Hey! I uh…what are you wearing

BRITT: Yeah, no, I know, I tried calling –

ELLIE: My *(holds up the phone.)*

BRITT: No, your house – I told your mom to tell you to call me back –

ELLIE: Yeah, she…She doesn't always tell me when you call, that's why you should call *(holds up the cell phone again.)* –

BRITT: I know, I'm sorry, I lost where I wrote it down and don't have that number memorized yet, I'm sorry, I tried, though, I tried. It was a. Kinda last minute thing

ELLIE: Ok well it's …fine, we can just

(ELLIE starts to go inside.)

BRITT: Wait. *(She grabs ELLIE's arm.)* I need to tell you something.

ELLIE: Yeah?

BRITT: I think… I'm in love
and I don't want it to be weird.
Because there's a chance, it could be weird.

(ELLIE stops, her heart fluttering, BRITT's still holding her arm, they're looking into one another's eyes.)

ELLIE: Oh yeah?

BRITT: Yeah. Because – it's Amber.

(ELLIE's heart cracks.)

ELLIE: Amber.

BRITT: Yeah

ELLIE: You're in love with Amber

BRITT: Yeah

(ELLIE finally shakes BRITT off her arm.)

ELLIE: But she's. She's a cheerleader

BRITT: I mean, not really, not right now, and Amber's different

ELLIE: That's what you said about Katie –

BRITT: But Amber's actually different, and I dunno, I just.
Fell in love // with her

ELLIE: After you said you would never again after, after Katie –

BRITT: Yeah but like, What does Never really mean, you know?

ELLIE: Right.

(An awkward beat.)

ELLIE: Well. Okay.

(ELLIE starts to head into the gym.)

BRITT: What

ELLIE: It's just. (. . . .) You fall in love a lot

BRITT: Didn't realize there was a limit

ELLIE: Penguins mate for life

BRITT: I'm not a penguin, I'm a human, person

ELLIE: Okay, never mind.

(Beat. It's huffy. It's awkward.)

BRITT: You do look really cool.

ELLIE: Yeah, I know.

(Another long beat.)

ELLIE: I just.
Woulda been something different.
I didn't realize –

BRITT: Just felt weird not telling you. Because I always tell you. And I wanted you to know.

(Ellie nods.)

BRITT: Hey, so, I'm gonna head in, grab some snacks, you want anything? Grab you some coffin cookies or something? I can see if they've got the cupcakes with the purple frosting -

ELLIE: I'm good.

BRITT: Okay. Well, if I see those cupcakes, I'll save you two.

(BRITT starts to leave. Stops.)

BRITT: Hey.
Do I look like.
Handsome?

ELLIE: You look great, Britt.

BRITT: No but. Do I look handsome?

ELLIE: Sure.

(BRITT breathes deep. Leaves. Some song starts to play something like You Were Meant for Me *by Jewel. ELLIE sits by the bleachers. She looks at her phone but she doesn't know what she's looking for. Looks at the dancers. Back at her phone. AMBER enters. She's wearing her Juliet costume. She approaches ELLIE.)*

AMBER: Dollar for your thoughts

ELLIE: Oh. Hi. Nice…costume, is that… the play?

AMBER: Yeah. Had to beg Sister Magdalene a little bit she said okay, so.

ELLIE: It's weird, Britt's wearing the Romeo costume

AMBER: Oh yeah, weird.

ELLIE: Maybe I shoulda worn my Mercutio costume, I dunno! I dunno.

(A small beat. AMBER nudges ELLIE.)

AMBER: Come on, dollar for your thoughts

ELLIE: You'll seriously give me a dollar if I tell you?

AMBER: Oh, no, it's just an expression

ELLIE: My grandpa says Penny

AMBER: Yeah but. That's sadder than a dollar

ELLIE: Yeah, I guess.

AMBER: So, come on. Tell me.

(Ellie really hesitates before saying:)

ELLIE: Sometimes my cellphone'll say Searching and I know it means for a signal but.
I dunno, I kinda.
Relate.
Which is so dumb, right?
To relate to a phone?
It doesn't even mean - That.

AMBER: That's what you were thinking about?

ELLIE: Yeah, I thought about lying? But then I didn't.

AMBER: I'm glad you didn't.

ELLIE: Thanks

(A nice moment between the two of them.)

AMBER: It's cool you have a cell phone

ELLIE: It's only for emergencies. Technically.
But sometimes Britt calls me on it so.
I like to hold it.
Just in case.

AMBER: My mom won't let me have one. But if she did, I'd give you my number.

ELLIE: Why?

AMBER: So you could call me. Duh.

ELLIE: Oh. Yeah, duh.

(Another beat.)

AMBER: Hey, uh. What were you gonna tell me the other day? About the play?

ELLIE: Oh, nothing. It's not important

AMBERL So? Tell me anyway.

(ELLIE fiddles with the phone. Decides to tell her.)

ELLIE: I just.
    So like, usually I have like.
    More lines and more things to do when I'm cast in a play
    but this part's smaller so I have more time to like.
    Really dig deep.
    And I was noticing that like.
    Mercutio is really upset about Romeo falling in love with Juliet
    and I know, I know it's like. Because she's a Capulet,
    but also he seems kinda, I dunno.
    Jealous?
    And I thought maybe,
    maybe it might be because
    Mercutio loves Romeo.

AMBER: Oh, shit.

ELLIE: Right?

AMBER: That actually,
    it makes sense.

ELLIE: Yeah.

AMBER: Like, a lot of sense.

ELLIE: Thanks.

(ELLIE smiles.)

ELLIE: So yeah, maybe I should've worn my costume, too

AMBER: I dunno, you look pretty good for a cheerleader

ELLIE: Well, I'm a dead cheerleader

AMBER: Not really, you're Undead

ELLIE: Basically the same thing

AMBER: Uh, not really!

ELLIE: It has the word Dead in it!

AMBER: Yeah but only a part of you's dead, not the whole of you

ELLIE: But the You that counts is the Dead part! You're eating brains!

AMBER: You wanna eat my brains?

ELLIE: Uh ew, no

AMBER: Are you sure? You can't like smell them through my skull?!

ELLIE: Oh my god, stop, you're being ridiculous

AMBER: Oooh maybe I'm turning, I think your zombie disease might be catching 'cause I think I can smell...

(AMBER does some sorta crazy sniffing thing and she can't smell brains but she can smell ELLIE's hair. She stops.)

ELLIE: Something wrong?

AMBER: No, nothing.
Nothing.
You just do look really pretty tonight

(BRITT comes up to AMBER, tugs at her arm.)

BRITT: Come on, we doing this or what?

AMBER: Oh yeah, for sure

(Amber lets herself be pulled away.)

ELLIE: Wait, what – What're you –

BRITT: You'll see

(ELLIE reaches out to grabs BRITT's arm but she only grasps the air

A song comes on, it's both sensual and like fast-beat sexual at the same time,
Something like a sick remix version of <u>My Heart Will Go On</u>

BRITT pulls AMBER to the center of the gym,
a spotlight on them,   (though we can see ELLIE off and watching)

They put their hands up so that their hands are touching,
        palm to palm
        holy palmers touch

    It's slow motion and dreamy,

a dream come true for BRITT,

a nightmare for ELLIE,

        a daydream for AMBER, who wishes her palms were touching another's

It's a little reminiscent of the sword fight,
        but isn't that, at the

*same time,
it's a little more sensual,
it's beautiful.*

They dance and dance until the lights go on, all the lights, every light in the building, it all goes on at once and the music disappears and we're thrown into the next scene.)

SCENE VIII: AFTERSHOCKS

(Monday morning after the dance, outside the Principal's office, ELLIE and BRITT are in the middle of a fight.)

ELLIE: I wouldn't've narc'ed!

BRITT: You so would have, either that or you would have tried to talk me outta it -

ELLIE: They're gonna pull the play, you know they're gonna pull it

BRITT: I didn't think – I thought if I dressed like Romeo they wouldn't have freaked out THAT much,

ELLIE: Yeah but you made them think about it, you shoved it in their faces and made them think about it! And now they realize that we're just a bunch of girls dressing up like girls and dressing up like guys and we're just sinfully sinning up a sin-storm in their shitty sinn-y minds, god, shit

BRITT: I was Romeo

ELLIE: They didn't see Romeo they saw Britt and Amber,

BRITT: But it wasn't –

ELLIE: Girl One and Girl Two

BRITT: I wasn't, I really, wasn't -

ELLIE: What're you talking about, wasn't what?

BRITT: I dunno!
   Because, like…because, I dunno, sometimes I do feel like Romeo.
   And sometimes I don't.
   Like, sometimes it's not pretending, sometimes I am.
   Him.
   For real,
   not the character but like. Him. And.
   Like to not have to be a girl for a while,
   for a minute, that was.
   It felt.
   Like, sometimes it's.
   Nice to not be She?
   (. . . .)
   Whatever, though, okay,
   Whatever, you're right,
   they didn't see that,
   they saw me and Amber and,
   that was the point anyway.
   I just
   Forgot it for a second because
   for a second I was Romeo.

(ELLIE doesn't know how to respond.)

ELLIE: We coulda done it together

BRITT: You don't get it, Ellie

ELLIE: What don't I get I don't get sticking it to the school, to the church I don't get just because you have a crush on her -

BRITT: Amber's bi,
   I'm gay,

> You're not.
> It's not the same

(Beat. This hurts.)

ELLIE: Right.
  Right, right.

BRITT: Come on, this wasn't your fight

ELLIE: Right, no, I know,
  I know, it didn't belong.
  To me.

(The door to the office opens and AMBER comes out. She's wearing the regular school uniform, not her cheer uniform.)

AMBER: Your turn.

BRITT: How bad…?

(AMBER just shakes her head and shrugs. BRITT sighs, leaves.)

AMBER: What're you doing here

ELLIE: Oh, you know. Support.

AMBER: Sure. It's not looking good

ELLIE: Shit.

AMBER: I know. I mean, what are we supposed to do, just put on plays that have only girls in them?! Do plays like that exist, even?!

ELLIE: I dunno

AMBER: This isn't like the first play that they've done where girls play guys! I don't know what the big deal is –

ELLIE: Oh yeah, if it wasn't a big deal then why'd you do it in the first place? You both knew what you were doing, shit. *(Beat)* Why aren't you wearing your uniform?

AMBER: Oh, I. Got kicked off the squad.

ELLIE: Seriously?

AMBER: Yeah, it…they said it's because I can't make up the lost time but. I know. (. . . .) Hey, but fuck it, we can still like. Do the play, though, together, like, guerilla style

ELLIE: Sure.

AMBER: We all already have the lines down,
we can make our own costumes, find like a parking lot to do it in!
Or maybe a storefront might be better -
wait, this is actually a really good idea, we can do all that because it's not like we can't do this, it's that they don't want us to do it while inside these stupid walls, but we can still do it!
Come on, whattaya say?

ELLIE: I don't wanna talk about it

AMBER: Why not?

ELLIE: Because. I don't wanna do the play anymore

AMBER: What, why?!

ELLIE: Because.

AMBER: But because WHY

ELLIE: Becausebecause BECAUSE
Because I'm not fucking straight,
Because I'm in love with Britt, okay?!
Jesus, fuck.

AMBER: I knew it

ELLIE: What the fuck, how'd you know?!

AMBER: No, I mean, I just,
I guessed it,
suspected it, I...
(beat)
So you're –

ELLIE: Something, I'm something.
I dunno what word, but I am
and I've never told anybody because I can't.
Because if you don't have a word for it,
what's the point of saying anything, because my mom –

(. . . .) It just sucks.
To constantly, I'm constantly,
my real self, it's there,
it's in me,
but I can't,
I'm hiding me,
I'm hiding me because I can't

AMBER: It looks like – it hurts to – hide, though

ELLIE: It does. But. It's better because I'm the only one hurting me.

AMBER: I don't like seeing you hurt

ELLIE: Oh well.

(Beat between them.)

AMBER: I'll See you.
   Now that I know?
   I'll See you.

ELLIE: I'd rather you didn't

AMBER: Oh, come on

ELLIE: I'd rather be invisible

AMBER: Well, you're not. You're not invisible, you're the opposite of invisible, you're –

ELLIE: Visible?

AMBER: You're You,
   You're so much you that it just radiates off you,
   And you fill up every space you're in just by being in it

(A beat. They see each other. The door opens and BRITT comes out. They look at her.

BRITT opens her mouth to speak but

The Sailor Moon *theme song starts playing*

BRITT starts doing a choreographed dance to the song.
ELLIE joins
AMBER joins

The three of them and this dance transfer us into -)

SCENE IX: SLEEPOVER

(Everything transforms into a bedroom. AMBER, ELLIE and BRITT are having a sleepover. It's got everything you need – cute pjs, music and alcohol. They're doing

that dance together but in real time. The three are having a sleepover at Amber's house. It's the Friday after the dance. The song ends.)

ELLIE: I fucking love Sailor Moon

AMBER: It's the fucking best

BRITT: Sailor Uranus and Neptune are so gay, you can't even tell me otherwise

AMBER: Yeah, everyone knows that, it's just like an obvious truth

BRITT: They're both so hot

ELLIE: You're hot

(ELLIE laughs loudly, takes a drink from the bottle of Malibu Rum that Amber's mom got for Christmas three years ago and never opened.)

AMBER: Come on, quit hogging it, share

(AMBER takes the bottle, sips.)

BRITT: Hey, I thought of one, I thought of one - Never Have I Ever failed French class

AMBER: Oh my god, that's so unfair!

BRITT: Well, I thought of one and now you have to drink!

ELLIE: Yeah, you're way too sober

AMBER: I thought we were done –

ELLIE: No, we were paused, we were Intermission-ing, drink, DRINK IT

(AMBER drinks.)

AMBER: Okay, okay - Never have I ever... gotten a cavity.

(ELLIE and BRITT both drink.)

ELLIE: I have so many cavities my mouth is like a cavity factory

AMBER: All my teeth are virgin teeth *(She smiles widely, showing her teeth.)*

BRITT: I didn't know teeth could be virgins

ELLIE: Does that mean I lost my virginity because my teeth lost their virginity by getting cavities

(They all laugh, it's ridiculous but also ELLIE is so drunk.)

ELLIE: Never have I ever stolen anything bigger than a snickers bar

AMBER: Wait, but how big a snickers bar

ELLIE: I dunno, a general sized snickers bar

AMBER: But they come in different sizes

ELLIE: Heyheyheyheywaithey

AMBER: What

ELLIE: They come in different sizes – that's.... what a sex joke is

(They all laugh.)

AMBER: Come on, we should stop

BRITT: It's my turn

AMBER: Okay, well do one that you know...nobody's done

(ELLIE's getting gross is what she means.)

BRITT: Right, okay, fine. Buzzkill. Never have I ever killed someone

(ELLIE takes a drink anyway.)

AMBER: You've killed someone?

ELLIE: I dunno, does a fish count as a person

BRITT: Obviously not

ELLIE: Isn't it weird like
Mercutio dies
and like
if they let us do the play,
I woulda been dying all the time!
Three nights in a row!
Mercutio – dead!

(ELLIE fake dies, dramatically.)

AMBER: Come on, we can play something else

ELLIE: A PLAGUE ON BOTH YOUR HOUSES
hahahha I woulda been so good, too

BRITT: We all woulda been great

ELLIE: A plague! *(She directs this directly to Britt and Amber.)* A PLAGUE!

(The mood has shifted. It feels almost dangerous.)

BRITT: All right, calm down!

ELLIE: never have I ever gotten a whole play banned because of a stupid thing I did at a school dance.

(Beat.)

ELLIE: Well, drink, why aren't you drinking

AMBER: Ellie, you wanna take it easy

ELLIE: I am taking it easy, I'm chill! So chill

BRITT: Come on, you're acting stupid

ELLIE: I'm not acting, I'm being normal

BRITT: Fine, you're literally being stupid, so stop -

ELLIE: Never have I ever gotten detention,
Never have I ever gotten into multiple fights in the halls of school.
Never have I ever cheated on someone I supposedly loved
Well?
You're not drinking

BRITT: That's a bitch move

ELLIE: So what, I guess I'm a bitch

AMBER: Let's get you to sleep

ELLIE: Mercutio was in love with Romeo, you know

BRITT: What are you talking about

ELLIE: He was, he was, it's like so obvious and you didn't even get that, you don't even –

(But whatever she's about to say doesn't come out. She runs out of the room. The sound of her vomiting fills the air. AMBER and BRITT share a look. BRITT's still really pissed. AMBER runs off after ELLIE.)

SCENE X: 4am

(Outside Amber's home, on a deck or a porch, something like that. AMBER sits outside. She's wearing a sweatshirt but it's still chilly, a blanket wrapped around her shoulders. We see BRITT behind the door. Hesitates before speaking.)

BRITT: Hey

AMBER: Oh, hey

BRITT: I was wondering where you were

AMBER: Just here.

BRITT: Cool.

(Awkward beat.)

BRITT: Do you mind if I.
    Can I like.
    Join? You?

AMBER: Oh, for sure.

(BRITT tentatively joins. Doesn't share the blanket. Does a cool lean and progressively gets closer to AMBER throughout.)

BRITT: Ellie finally stop vomiting?

AMBER: Oh yeah, a while ago.

BRITT: It was nice of you to hold her hair.

AMBER: Yeah, well.
   (. . . .)
   I love listening to the crickets.
   They sound like music.
   Sorry, that's.
   Probably doesn't make sense –

BRITT: Nah, I get it.
   They do.

(They sit and listen to the crickets sing.)

AMBER: You think they're singing?
   Or like.
   Know the songs they're making?

BRITT: I dunno.
   Maybe they're saying cheers

AMBER: Nah

BRITT: Yeah, chanting cheers!

AMBER: Crickets aren't cheerleaders

BRITT: You don't know that!
   They can be like
   Gimme an A!
   Gimme a X!
   Gimme a Q!

AMBER: What are you spelling

BRITT: Well, I dunno, I don't think crickets spell words the same way we do

AMBER: You're crazy

BRITT: Probably don't even speak words the way we do!
   So who are we to say what they're saying

AMBER: I guess that makes sense.

(They listen to the crickets.)

BRITT: Why aren't you asleep?

AMBER: Oh.
I dunno.
It's nothing –
I'm usually awake this late.
Have trouble like.
Being asleep.

BRITT: Oh.
Well.
Sleeping's like.
My favorite thing to do so.
Cannot relate.
(Does something nerdy and weird and endearing.)

AMBER: You're awake now

BRITT: Yeah, well. The floor was hard.

(beat)

AMBER: My thoughts itch my brain too much to sleep.
Or dream, even.
So I usually stay awake.
Listening to the crickets sing.

(They listen to the crickets sing.)

AMBER: My dad.
We used to listen to this song,
when I was little,
it was in French.
And like, I hate French,
like, in class?
I'll never speak it for real.

and I don't understand French when it's being sung,
Like, at all,
Like, not even a little,
But that song,
I got what it was about.
All sad and heartbreak
But a little bit of hope
And that's what I hear when I listen to the crickets sing, I think.

BRITT: Right. Or. They're going Be Aggressive! Be Be Aggressive!

(AMBER does laugh at that. A breeze, BRITT shivers.)

AMBER: You cold?

BRITT: Yeah, a little.

AMBER: Here, grab some blanket

BRITT: You sure? I don't wanna hog -

AMBER: Yeah, it'll be warmer with both of us under it anyway.

(BRITT hesitates, then places the blanket half-heartedly over her shoulder.)

AMBER: Come on, take more!

(AMBER puts the blanket fully around her, too, so they're both enveloped in the blanket together, huddling against one another for warmth.)

BRITT: This is nice

AMBER: Yeah.

BRITT: I like – the way you talk about things. I like it.

(The sound of birds starting to chirp.)

BRITT: Birds

AMBER: We talked away the night.
   (. . . .)

   .
   I don't think that birds sing.
   I think they're talking.
   Saying mundane shit
   Like, Hi, hello, how are you today

BRITT: And gossiping about their bird neighbors

AMBER: Or like their squirrel neighbors

BRITT: Or us!

AMBER: Oh, for sure like 'What the hell're those random girls doing?'

BRITT: Yeah, what are they, in love or something?

(Awkward moment.)

BRITT: Birds are weird

AMBER: Yeah, they are. They really are.

(Another few seconds of listening to birds. AMBER shifts a little bit away from BRITT.)

BRITT: Do you think birds can like
   Kiss

AMBER: Probably not

BRITT: Oh

AMBER: Yeah. They don't have lips.

BRITT: Right.

(Another few seconds, AMBER shifts away from BRITT a little.)

BRITT: Do you need lips to kiss?

AMBER: Oh.
   I guess.
   I dunno.
   I never really.
   Thought of it before.

BRITT: I dunno
   I dunno

*(BRITT is about to go for a kiss, leans closer and closer
      but AMBER moves her head away,
      pretends not to notice BRITT's lips catching air.
A moment where they both sit in that awkward silence.)*

BRITT: Hey, I'm. I'm just gonna go – get a – it's cold, so I need to get a – sweatshirt or -

AMBER: Okay

*(BRITT leaves. AMBER is still out there, listening to the birds.
   She stands, the blanket around her shoulder like a cape.
Hums a little bit of "La Vie en Rose".
   Dances with an invisible partner, humming the song.
ELLIE comes out, bleary-eyed and headache-y
She's wearing a sweater, is wrapped in a throw blanket.)*

AMBER: Hey! You're alive!

ELLIE: What time is it, is it one thousand o'clock, I can't believe I'm awake and I feel this shitty

AMBER: Yeah, too bad you can't be like Sleeping Beauty until it wears off

ELLIE: Yeah. I brushed my teeth for like a million years, that helped a little.

(beat)

AMBER: How'd you sleep?

ELLIE: I dunno, but I guess I did. Somehow.

(beat)

ELLIE: So. Dollar for your thoughts.

AMBER: You don't have a dollar

ELLIE: I wouldn't give you my dollar if you begged me but I still want your thoughts.

(small beat)

AMBER: I miss cheer.

ELLIE: The falling?

AMBER: Yeah.
But like.
Not the team.

ELLIE: Mmm.

AMBER: Not the – people

ELLIE: Right

AMBER: They kinda actually.
   They suck.
   They're so.
   Fake.
   Like acting is fake but also more real than all of them.

ELLIE: Yeah.

AMBER: I wish we could've done the play.

ELLIE: It sucks because you didn't even get to
   experience the best parts

AMBER: Like what?

ELLIE: Like, I dunno,
   getting like scared because you're afraid you'll forget
   a line or a cue or mess up a quick change
   but also it's like
   inside jokes? And like talking backstage while we wait
   to go on
   and you don't even know, you don't even KNOW,
   sometimes after tech we go to the Friendly's by the
   abandoned Cheesecake Factory and order mozzarella
   sticks and strawberry sundaes,
   they have the best mozzarella sticks

AMBER: Oh. I usually go to the Friendly's by

ELLIE: The Glenbury Mall, yeah, no that one's TRASH
   this one's better
   because it's ours.
   And by the time we're doing it for real in front of an
   audience, we're all so like.
   Together.
   And it feels like it'll last that way forever
   but it never does.
   I dunno why, but it never lasts.

(The birds are getting louder. Dawn is warming. Their heads are getting closer.)

AMBER: I never noticed

ELLIE: Yeah?

AMBER: You.
    Have a scar.

ELLIE: Oh

AMBER: Right there

ELLIE: Yeah. I know.

AMBER: Right

ELLIE: I mean, sometimes I forget.
    Don't keep track of all my scars, you know.

(Their heads are getting closer.)

ELLIE: You smell like lemons

AMBER: Yeah

ELLIE: What do I smell like
    besides like…sweaty booze armpit

AMBER: You.
    You just.
    You smell like you.

ELLIE: Is that gross?

AMBER: No.
    It's not.
    It's really, really not.
    I can't describe it.
    Because if I were to describe it,
    I'd have to talk about your eyes.

And your pores.
And the hair inside your nostrils.
And all the things that make you You
Are all the things that I can and can't see
That's what you smell like.
And like,
you're always here,
Inside me,
Keeping my dreams awake
And I can't sleep
Because when I sleep I dream of you
And when I wake up and the dream shatters
into splinters and shards that I can't even see,
All those invisible splinters and shards enter me and cut me open
And I don't know what to do with any of that
And I know what you smell like but what do you taste like
And what is a kiss, anyway,
I don't think we think about that enough,
What is a kiss

(AMBER leans in, kisses ELLIE,
ELLIE hesitates but kisses her back,
they kiss one another
BRITT appears, now wearing a hoodie.
Sees.)

BRITT: Oh. Okay.

ELLIE: Britt, no, wait

BRITT: What the hell are you doing, experimenting?

AMBER: It's not an experiment

ELLIE: Shut up, Amber!

AMBER: I don't like you like that, Britt! Don't be mad at Ellie

ELLIE: I don't need you to defend me!

AMBER: I wasn't defending you, I was just saying –

ELLIE: I don't want you to say anything

AMBER: But you kissed me back

BRITT: I just can't believe you would with. You knew.

(BRITT starts walking away.)

ELLIE: Britt, Britt no, stop, wait!

(BRITT stops, back to ELLIE. ELLIE searches for what to say. Finally blurts out:)

ELLIE: Mercutio loved Romeo

BRITT: That's so stupid

ELLIE: Why

AMBER: It's not in the play

ELLIE: But it is.
Because Mercutio loved Romeo.
He was just
simply
head over heels in deep down LOVE with Romeo.
Like, they were best friends and made up games and picked flowers and made it rain fallen leaves in the Autumn and
created a whole world that belonged to the two of them,
just the two of them,
nestled inside of the bigger world, obviously, the one full of other people,
they had their own world.

A whole entire earth that was only big enough for the two of them to fit inside.
But then as they got older,
Mercutio started to notice things,
little things like
How the sun made Romeo's eyes glow different
or How his laugh shook through him like the waves of an ocean,
and it made Mercutio's breath get caught in his throat
and Mercutio started to bend towards him,
You know, like how plants bend towards the sun?
He started to bend towards him
because Romeo was his sun.

.

But then Romeo,
His Suns were
Not Mercutio.
They were Rosalind and
Juliet and.
Why does it have to be Juliet?
You know?

.

Why does he love Juliet
when Mercutio's been there all along?

(A long moment of silence. None of them really know what to do.)

AMBER reaches out to grab ELLIE's hand but ELLIE pulls away.)

ELLIE: No, I'm – Sorry, sorry, I shouldn't have [kissed you]

(AMBER looks at ELLIE. We watch her heart breaking.)

BRITT: How was I supposed to know?

ELLIE: Would it have made a difference? If I told you I loved you?

*(BRITT doesn't know what to say.
Because no.
It wouldn't have made a difference.
They just look at one another,
Passing that revelation back and forth.)*

ELLIE: I know.
   I know

*(They all sit in that moment for a moment. Time stops.
They turn away from us.)*

EPILOGUE

(When they turn back, it's time skipping forward, moving forward, because life, it goes on. They each stand in separate areas of the space, facing us, never looking at one another.)

AMBER: Countdown to graduation!

BRITT: Oh, shit, I got into MIT!

ELLIE: Gonna stay and work at Starbucks for

AMBER: going to school out in LA!

BRITT: Pledging at a

ELLIE: Double shot of

AMBER: got cast as Laura in the Glass Menagerie !

BRITT: changed my major, getting a Masters in

ELLIE: my classes will transfer over and

AMBER: oh, I used to cheer a million years ago

BRITT: big interview with a firm out in

ELLIE: only took five years but finally got my

AMBER: He's just a friend

BRITT: I think they're the one

ELLIE: she's pretty great

AMBER: he makes me happy

BRITT: they're definitely the one

ELLIE: I'm planning on proposing in a few

AMBER: I told him yes!

BRITT: I'm going to wear a suit

ELLIE: Say yes to the dress!

AMBER: Got a promotion!

BRITT: laid off

ELLIE: fired, but that's okay, I'm gonna start my own

AMBER: Doritos aren't chips

BRITT: We're having a baby!

ELLIE: We got a dog!

AMBER: I'm gonna be a mom!

BRITT: I used to have this friend, a million years ago

ELLIE: Oh, well, forever didn't last

AMBER: caught him cheating in the

BRITT: What color anniversary is this

ELLIE: I love the smell of Lemons

AMBER: got a parakeet at least

BRITT: birds don't sing, they talk

ELLIE: Oh yeah, I did Romeo and Juliet, like a million years ago

AMBER: Well, we were supposed to but actually

BRITT: it got cancelled

ELLIE: Banned

AMBER: I was Juliet, if you can imagine

BRITT: Romeo

ELLIE: Mercutio - he's the harder part, you know

AMBER: Oh Romeo

BRITT: Holy Palmers –

ELLIE: A plague!

AMBER: I was good

BRITT: I remember

ELLIE: I can remember

AMBER: There was this one time

BRITT: this one girl

ELLIE: my best friend, I think about

AMBER: Her name was Ellie

BRITT: I still think about her

ELLIE: All the time

AMBER: Yeah, I think about her

BRITT: first real love, I think

ELLIE: someone I really loved, I remember

AMBER: I can remember

BRITT: I still think

ELLIE: remember

AMBER: think about

BRITT: I think

ELLIE: she was

AMBER: I really loved

BRITT: someone I

ELLIE: I loved

AMBER: she was

BRITT: I really loved

ELLIE: someone I

AMBER: think about her

BRITT: all the time

ELLIE: all the time

AMBER: O,

Blackout.

End of play.

More Great Plays Available From Original Works Publishing

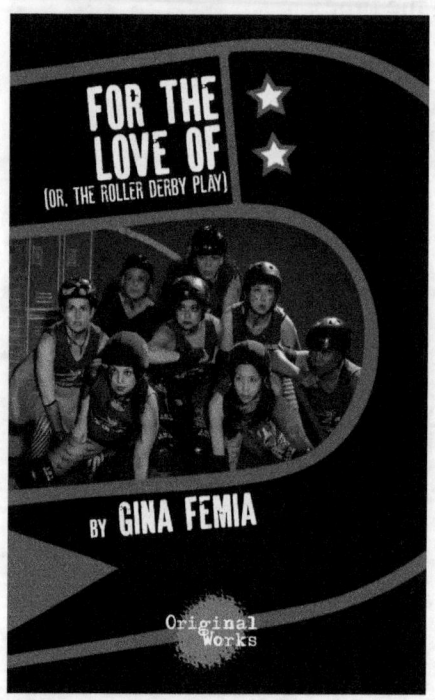

FOR THE LOVE OF (or, The Roller Derby Play)
By Gina Femia

Synopsis: When Joy gets on the Brooklyn Scallywags and meets the star, Lizzie Lightning, she and her long term partner Michelle find their lives turned upside down. For The Love Of asks how much you're willing to sacrifice – or lose – in order to follow your heart.

Cast Size: 9 Diverse Females

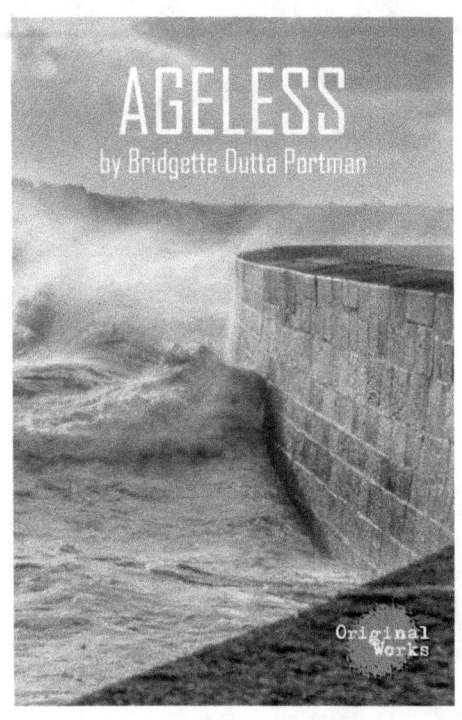

AGELESS by Bridgette Dutta Portman

Synopsis: Ninety is the new thirty at the turn of the 22nd century. When Marin refuses to take the anti-aging drug celebrated by the rest of society, she invokes her mother's ire and risks becoming marginalized in a culture that worships youth, denies death, and treats old age as a malady. As Marin's choice begins to affect not only her but the people she loves, will she find the strength to hold out, or succumb to social pressure?

Cast Size: 4 Females, 2 Males, 4 Various

AGLAONIKE'S TIGER by Claudia Barnett
Synopsis: Aglaonike, the first female astronomer, could predict lunar eclipses, but her science was suspect because she was a woman. She therefore billed herself as a sorceress and claimed she could draw down the moon. Inspired by her unsung history, this coming-of-age play follows the protagonist through a series of challenges, both magical and scientific. Drawing on ancient Greek traditions and postmodern performance trends, Aglaonike's Tiger is stylized and visual and uses puppets and masks to explore political, ecological, and scientific themes.
Cast Size: 5 Women, 1 Male

YOU ARE WHAT YOU by Mora V. Harris

Synopsis: Competitive eater Francie is desperate to find a way to help her younger sister Trisha eat. When celebrity chef Electra Sinclair arrives on their doorstep, she thinks she may have found just the thing to set Trisha on the road to recovery. Yet Trisha's illness worsens as she begins seeing visions of a talking Pot Roast, and Francie becomes distracted by an ex hell-bent on exploiting her in a cogent work of non-fiction. The sisters struggle to take care of each other and nourish themselves in this comedy about learning from the things we crave.

Cast Size: 5 Women

NOTES

NOTES

www.ingramcontent.com/pod-product-compliance
Lightning Source LLC
LaVergne TN
LVHW022323080426
835508LV00041B/2529